The Largest Water Conservancy Pivotal Project in the World

The Magnificent Three Gorges Project

黄河水利出版社

Preface

Yangtze River is the most beautiful river around the world. It has 200km long natural art gallery, and 7000 year's culture accumulation. Before the construction of the Three Gorges Project (TGP), the grand natural sight and torrential river stimulus give people deep impressions about the Three Gorges. While today, with the construction of the TGP, when we mention the Three Gorges again, people will recall Chairman Mao's poem that "modify the Yangtze river to a lake". It is a dream of all the Chinese to construct the TGP, improve the navigation of the Three Gorges reach, and impose water resources of the Three Gorges. This project will benefit all of the Chinese people. With the construction of this project, this dream will come true soon.

From June 1st, 2003, the TGP began to impound; June 16th of the same year, trial navigation of the double way 5-flight ship locks succeed. June 24, the first hydraulic Turbine Units began to work. From that time on, we have gained integrative benefit from the TGP according to the designed functions. With gigantic storage capacity, flood from upriver will not disturb people in the area of the middle and lower reaches of the Yangtze River. When the water of the Yangtze River runs through the TGP, the generators generate powers to support the modernization of China without intervals. From that tome on, there is no riptide or jam in the Three Gorges waterway. It is possible for 10,000-ton barge fleet to sail upstream from Shanghai to the harbors of Chongqing directly. The waterway of Yangtze River will become real gold waterway.

The Three Gorges Project has attracted most attention from home and abroad. It has the following reasons: the TGP has integrative benefit on the aspect of flood control; power generation and navigation. On the other hand it has a gigantic investment, and it mixes many complex problems. For example, it is built on a complex geologic area near the Wu Mountain. It will inundate natural sight and historical sites under the 175m water level. It will inundate 2 cities, 11 counties and 1771 countries; this will make millions of people move out their hometown.

In a word, the Three Gorges Project will attract us all the time from its construction to its running. Because it mixes profit and harm together. This project will have a close relation with us forever.

Facing to this grand project, it is beyond our ability to judge its result, but we have duty to record the development of this project. At the turning point of the Three Gorges changing from river to lake, we have to witness these changes. This book will show you the Three Gorges Project with words and pictures. We will introduce the natural sight, environmental and historical site impacts of this project. We know that the world famous TGP and the Three Gorges cannot be described with this tiny words and pictures. If you want to feel the grandness of TGP and the beauty of the Three Gorges, you'd better come, and enjoy it by yourself.

For workers of the Three Gorges Project!

For people move out of their hometown in reservoir area!
For friends who loves the Three Gorges!
For the originators who brought culture here!
For the grandness Three Gorges Project!
For the eternal Three Gorges!

Editors   Li jinlong

Contents

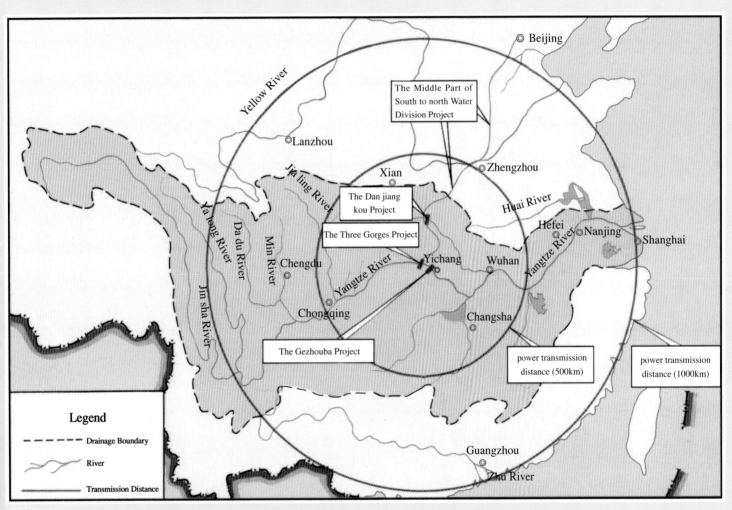

Sketch Map of Electricity Transmission Scope of the Three Gorges Water Conservancy Pivotal Project

The magnificent three gorges project

Walls of stones will stand upstream to the west.
To hold back Wushan clouds and rain.
Till a smooth lake rise in the narrow gorges.

The silver dam of the TGP

A smooth lake rises in the narrow gorges

The TGP reservoir area after impounding

Modern poems on the three gorges

Mao zedong

Swimming

-To the tune of shui diao ge tou

I have just drunk the waters of changsha
And come to eat the fish of wuchang,
Now i am swimming across the great yangtze,
Looking afar to the open sky of chu,
Let the wind blow and waves beat,
Better far than jdly strolling in a courtyard,
Today i am at ease,
"It was by a stream that the master said-
Thus do things flow away!"

Sails move with the wind.
Tortoise and snake are still,
Great plans are afoot:
A bridge will fly to span the north and south,
Turning a deep chasm into a thoroughfare;
Walls of stone will stand upstream to the west
Till a smooth lake rises in the narrow gorges.
The mountain goddess if she is still there
Will marvel at a world so changed.

The Yangtze River is a water resource treasury, after completing the TGP,
this resource can be fully exploited and used

水调歌头

游泳

才饮长沙水，又食武昌鱼。万里长江横渡，极目楚天舒。不管风吹浪打，胜似闲庭信步，今日得宽馀。子在川上曰：逝者如斯夫！

风樯动，龟蛇静，起宏图。一桥飞架南北，天堑变通途。更立西江石壁，截断巫山云雨，高峡出平湖。神女应无恙，当惊世界殊。

毛泽东

一九五六年六月

The Three Gorges Water Conservancy Pivotal Project after the first stage of impounding

The Grand Three Gorges Project

There is a silver dam on the Xiling Gorge's reach of the Three Gorges. It is the Three Gorges Project. The construction of the Three Gorges Project is an action of human beings to modify the nature. In the year 1919, Dr. Sun Yat-sen assumed to exploit water resource of the Yangtze River. In 1956, Chairman Mao Zedong, described blueprint of the Three Gorges Project. On April 3, 1992, the national people's congress passed the resolution on the Construction of the Three Gorges Project. On November 8, 1994, the Three Gorges Project started constructing. On June 2003, the Three Gorges Project began impounding, the dam is open to navigation, and the first group of generators began to put out electric power. The Three Gorges is gradually changing from river to lake. The whole construction of the TGP will be completed in 2009.

The Three Gorges Project is the largest water conservancy pivotal project in the world today. It consists of dam, the powerhouse, the spillway, and navigation structures. The dam is 2 335meters long, 115meters wide at the bottom, 40meters wide on the top, with the crest at elevation 185meters. The navigation structure consists of twin 5-flight ship locks and one step vertical shoplift. The ship locks are treated as the fourth gorges on the Yangtze River. It is a dug trough in granite mountain. The trough is 6 442 meters long and 176 meters deep. The ship lock is built on the basis of it. It is the ship lock with the most flights and highest water head (113m) all over the world. The vertical ship lift can handle 11,800tons ship totally. The powerhouse will be equipped with 32 units of generator of 7×10^5 kW each, with a total capacity of 2.24×10^7 kWh. The main work quality to be done in the construction for principle structures and division works is as follows: earth and rock excavation is $1.0283 \times 10^8 m^3$, earth and rock embankment is $3.198 \times 10^7 m^3$, concrete placing is $2.794 \ 10^7 m^3$, rebar is 4.63×10^5 tons, and metal works is 2565×10^2 tons the principle structure's concrete placement once reached $5.48 \times 10^6 m^3$ per year. The peak excavation reached $3 \times 10^7 m^3$ per year, embanking intensity reached $2.8 \times 10^6 m^3$. All these intensities have made a new world record of dam construction.

With a wide range of integrative profit of flood control, power generation and navigation, the Three Gorges Project (TGP) is a criteria project of exploiting the Yangtze River. The total storage capacity is $393 \times 10^8 m^3$, it is three times over the Dongting Lake's capacity, with $221.5 \times 10^8 m^3$ flood control capacity. This can effectively control the flood from upstream of the Yangtze River. The Jingjiang River's flood control capacity is raised from 10-year frequency to the 100-year frequency. The things running in the Yangtze River is not waters but coal and oil. Before the power generation of the TGP, the water resources of the Yangtze River are wasted. TGP will supply 1000×10^8 KWH clear power. Compared with the same output thermal power plants, it will equal to the reduction of 5×10^7 tons raw coal combustion annually, which means 1.2×10^8 tons CO_2, 2×10^6 tons SO_2, 10 thousand tons CO, 3.7×10^5 tons NOx, and a large amount of waste water and solid discharge will be decreased correspondingly. This will beneficial to improvement of the environment of middle and east china, especially for prevention of acid rain damage and greenhouse affect. This clear and cheap power will support the modernization of China without interval.

The Magnificent Three
Gorges Project

The Magnificent Three Gorges Project

List of Principle Indices of the TGP

Item Description	Unit	Index	Item Description	Unit	Index
Reservoir					
Normal pool level	m	175	Flood Control Level	m	145
Dry Season Control Level	m	155	Flood Level in 1000 Year Frequency	m	175
Total Storage Capacity (under 175 meter)	m^3	393×10^8	Flood Control Capacity	m^3	221.5×10^8
Control Store Capacity	m^3	165×10^8	Control Runoff in Dry Season	m^3	5 860
Length of improved water course	km	660	Drainage Area	km^2	100×10^4
Reservoir Inindation	km^2	632	Surface Area	km^2	1 084
Major Construction and Equipment					
Dam Type		Concrete Gravity	Crest Elevation	m	185
Powerhouse Type		Dam-toe powerhouse	Max. Height	m	175
Installed Capacity	kw	$1\ 820 \times 10^4$	Number of units	set	26
Underground Powerhouse on the Rihgt Bank	kw	420×10^4	Number of units	set	6
Unit Capacity	kw	70×10^4	Ave. Power Generation	kwh	847×10^8
Permanent Shiplock		Double Way 5 Stage	Dimension of Chamber	mxmxm	280 x 34 x 5
Vertical Shiplock		One Way, 1 Stage	Dimension of Container	mxmxm	120 x 18 x 3.5
Reservoir Inundation					
Farm Land	hm^2	2.1×10^4	Orchard Land	hm^2	0.73×10^4
Population (1992 Index)		84.62×10^4	Population of Resettlement		113×10^4
Construction					
Earth & rock Excavation	m^3	$10\ 259 \times 10^4$	Earth & rock Embankment	m^3	$2\ 933 \times 10^4$
Concrete Placement	m^3	$2\ 715 \times 10^4$	Re-bar	t	35.43×10^4
Menal Works	t	28.08×10^4	Total Construction Duration	Year	17

The capacity of the underground powerhouse is excluded

Comparison on Main Technical Parameter of TGP and Similar Project Abroad

Country	Name	River	Installed Capacity (x10⁴KW)	Ave Power Generation x10⁸kwh	Max.Head M	Year of Generation
China	Three Gorges	Yangtze River	1 820	847	113	2003
Brazil and Paraguay	Itaipu	Parana River	1 260	710	123	1984
U.S.A	Grand Coulee	Columbia River	1 083	203	108	1942
Venezuela	Guri	Caroni River	1 030	510	146	1968
Brazil	Tucurui	Tocantins River	800	324	68	1984
Russia	Sayano-Shushensk	Yenisey River	640	237	220	1978
Russia	Klasnoyalsk	Yenisey River	600	204	100.5	1968
Canada	La Grande II	La Grande River	533	358	143	1979
Canada	Churchill Falls	Churchill River	523	345	322	1971

The capacity of the underground powerhouse is excluded

Dam Site

The dam site for TGP is selected at Sandouping of Yichang city of Hubei province. The total water catchments area hereof is about 100×10^4 km^2 with 4500×10^8 m^3 of average annual runoff.

The dam site for TGP is the best site for hydraulic power plants of the world. Around the Three Gorges area, there is only sound and intact granite with 70 km long and 30 km wide at Sandouping area. Some hydraulicsts joked that this area is chosen by God to construct TGP.

Here at the location of Sandouping dam site, the river valley is relatively open and broad, and there is a small islet called Zhongbaodao in the river, which is favorable for phased construction. This islet divided the Yangtze River into two parts one is 900 meter wide the other is 300meter wide. The axis of the transverses cofferdams is on this islet. With this good landform, it can be convenient to built this dam and reduce a great amount of capital.

The bedrock of this water conservancy pivotal project is sound and intact granite with 100MPa of compressive strength. The Fault and fissures in the bedrock are less

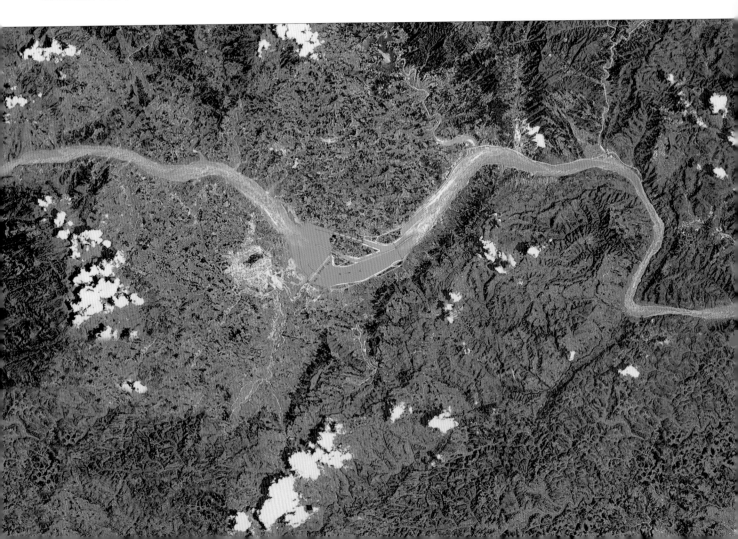

developed and most of them are well cemented. The permeability of the rock mass is slight in nature. The weathered layer in the hill on both side are a bit thick, ranging from 20 to 40 m, while few layers exist on the main river channel. In the vicinity of about 15 km around the dam site, there are no major disadvantageous geologic structures. The regional seismic activities are small in intensity, low in frequency. The whole area of dam site belongs to a slight seismic area ranking as degree VI of seismic classified by the state authority department concerned. The main building of the conservancy pivotal project is constructed on the basis

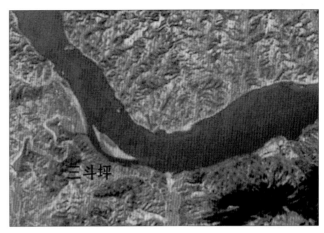

The Three Gorges Project Dam Site–Zhongbaodao

of degree VII of seismic.

There are 38 km valleys at lower reaches of the river. In order to make full use of TGP, the Gezhouba project will be used to compensate the navigation and power generation benefit.

TGP has a good outside communication. There are many railways to Yichang. There already exist direct accesses by a low-standard highway and waterway to the dam site. And a 26 km long expressway from Yichang to the dam site and 4 km long bridge on the Yangtze River have been constructed and opened to traffic in Oct. 1996, and several docks have been constructed in the dam site area.

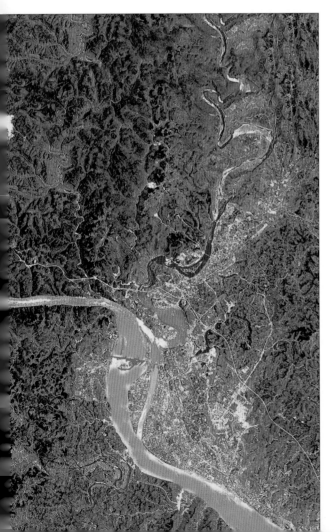

The three Gorges Flight Stages Hydraulic power Generation Station consists of TGP dam and Gezhouba Project. The dam site is located at Sandouping in the middle of Xiling Gorge. The bedrock of the site is sound and hard granite. It is the ideal site to construct a dam of the world.

The Sketch Map of the Location of the Three Gorges Project

Tianzhu Mountain Tunnel

The Liantuo Bridge

◄ Xiling Yangtze Bridge

Layout of the Project

The conservancy pivotal project of TGP consists of three major structures, including the dam, the powerhouses and the navigation facilities.

The dam is of a concrete gravity type. The total length of the dam axis is 2335 m 40 m wide on the top, 115 m wide at the bottom, the crest elevation at 185 m.

The spillway dam, which is located in the middle of the river course, is 483 m long in total, where there are 23 bottom outlet and 22 surface sluice gates. The dimensions of the bottom outlets are 7×9 m, with the elevation of the inlets at 90 m. The net width of the surface sluice gates is 8 m. with a maximum discharge capacity of 102,500m³/s, the project is able to discharge the possible maximum flood (PMF).

The powerhouses are placed on both sides of the spillway at the toe of the dam. It contains the right bank powerhouse and the left bank powerhouse. There will be 14 sets of hydraulic turbine generator units installed in the left bank and 12 sets on the right. These 26 sets of hydraulic turbine generator units in total (the hydraulic turbine is Francis type), 700 MW for each. On the right bank, there are 6 hydraulic turbine generator units with 700 MW in the underground powerhouse. There are 32 sets of hydraulic turbine generations on TGP.

The navigation structures consist of the double-way and five step flight locks and a shiplift. These are all located on the left bank side. The ship lock has the most complex structure and the highest water head over the world. Each lock chamber is dimensioned at $280 \times 34 \times 5$m (length × width × minimum water depth) capable of passing 10,000-ton barge fleet.

The vertical shiplift is designed as a one stage hoisting type with a ship container sized 120m × 18m × 3.5m,capable of carrying one 3000 ton passenger or cargo boat to the maximum 113meter. It is located on the right of the shiplock. This is also the most gigantic and complex shiplift over the world.

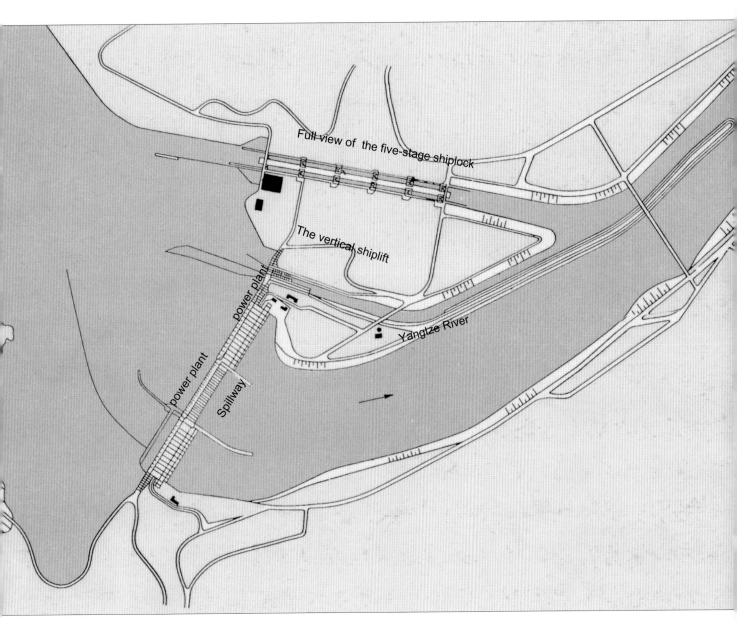

Full view of the five-stage shiplock

The vertical shiplift

power plant

power plant

power plant

Spillway

Yangtze River

Layout of the Three Gorges Project

The magnificent three gorges project

The Origngal Look of TGP Site

Construction Planning and Scheduling

The total duration of construction will last 17 years, it is divided into three stages.

In the first stage, after starting construction in 1993, the sub-river on the right side of the islet is enclosed, by taking advantage of the islet to build earth- and rock- fill cofferdam. Excavation to the granite, and concrete open division channel is built .the construction of the temporary shiplock on the left bank and open channel is completed. On Nov.8, 1997, the Yangtze River is closed.

In the second stage, from the year 1998, after the second stage earth- and rock- fill cofferdam is completed, the construction of the spillway, the intake dam and the power plant on the left bank is undergone. The first sets of generators are installed. Simultaneously, the permanent shiplock and shiplift is constructed on the left bank. In this stage, the ships go through the open division channel, or temporary shiplock. From June 1st, 2003, the TGP began to impound; June 16th of the same year, trial navigation of the twin 5-flight ship locks succeed. June 24, the first hydraulic Turbine Units began to work.

In the third stage, from the tear 2004 to 2009, at the end of the year 2004, the left dam with 1600m wide is completed, and the project crest elevation is reached 105m. In Oct. 2006, the length of the whole dam will reach 2039 m, and reach the planned crest elevation 185m. The third stage includes installation 12 sets hydraulic turbine generators on the right bank and 6 underground the right bank. In the year 2009, the whole project will be completed.

The Three Gorges Project Under Construction

The three gorges project
under construction

The Three Gorges Project
Under construction

Night View of the Three
Gorges Project

Fundamental Construction

The Second River Closure
of the TGP

Diversion channel is 3700 meters long and 350 meters wide, it takes the responsibility of navigation of the Yangtze River and flood sluice. On November 6, 2002, the diversion channel is successfully closed; the power plant on the right bank will stay on it.

The Three Gorges Project
Under Construction

Night View of the Three Gorges Project

Flood Control

TGP is the most important project functioning as a backbone in flood control system to protect the area sin the middle and lower reaches of the Yangtze River. The climate in the Three Gorges is monsoon like climate. The runoff of the Yangtze River from June to September, the flood season of the Yangtze River, is 70% to 75% of that of the whole year. According to the historical record, from the Han Dynasty (185 BC) to the later Qing Dynasty (1911AD), flood broke out in the Yangtze River 214 times, i.e. 1 time per ten years. While from the year 1921, cataclysm broke out 11 times, i.e. one time per six years. The cataclysms threaten the safety of 1.5 million ha plantation in the area of the Lake Dongting and Jianghan plain, 15 million people's life and treasure, and the railways from Beijing to Guangzhou and From Beijing to Kowloon.

There are three reasons cause the cataclysm in the middle and lower reaches of the Yangtze River. The first one is the flood of the whole drainage area. The second reason is the flood from the upstream which is caused by rainstorm of the Jinshajiang River, Mingjiang River JialingjiangRiver, Tuojing River, Wujiang River and Upstream of the Yangtze River area. The third reason is the flood from the middle and lower reaches of the Yangtze River. According to the field survey, no matter what kind of flood is, the main component of the flood is the flood from the upstream of the Yangtze River.

TGP is a backbone project in flood control system to protect the area in the middle and lower reaches of the Yangtze River. The normal pool level is 175 m, the total storage capacity is 393×10^8 m^3. In every year's flood season, the pool level will be reduced to the flood control level (145m). this can empty 221.5×10^8 m^3 storage capacity to store flood from the upstream, according to demand of flood control. In this way, after flood run through the dam, it will be reduced by 30 percent to effectively control the flood of the Yangtze River from the upstream to the middle and lower reaches.

With the flood control storage capacity of the reservoir, the Jinjiang River Section will be able to raise its flood control capacity from the present 10-year frequency to the 100-year. Even should a 1000-year frequency or like the flood in the year 1870, the vast plaints on both sides of this river section with the regulation of TGP and the assistance of appropriate operation of the flood diversion and retention works, would be kept from destruction which might occur due to the breaching of the main levees along the section without TGP. The flood disaster in the area of the middle and lower reaches of the Yangtze River and threat of flooding to Wuhan Municipality would be mitigated. And so would it create favorable conditions for a thorough rehabilitation and improvement of the Dongting Lake area.

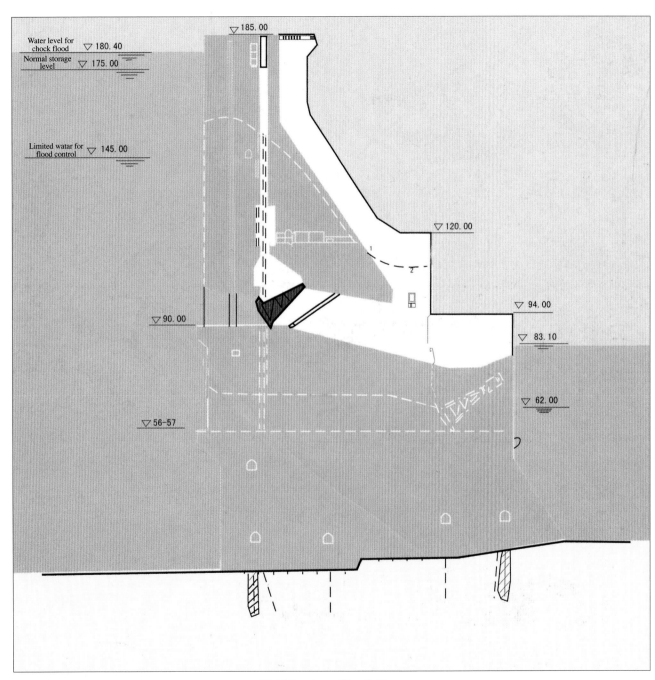

Right Section of the Spillway

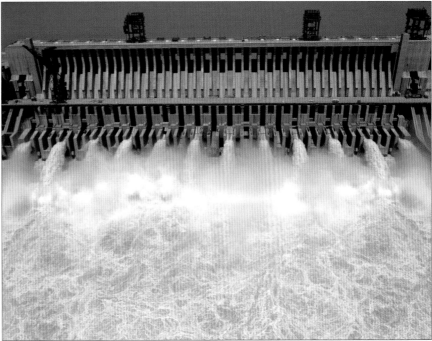

Flood Discharge from the priject

Flood Discharge from the priject

53

Power Generation

TGP's power station is the largest powerhouse around the world nowadays. Two powerhouses are placed at the toe of the dam. These two powerhouses are located at two sides of the spillway dam with total length of 1,210m. The total length of the powerhouse on the left is 643 m, with 14 sets of hydraulic turbine generator units installed, while that of one on the right, 576 m in total length, 12 hydraulic turbine generator units installed. There are 26 sets of hydraulic turbine generator units in total, 70×10^{4x}kw for each, totaling 1820×10^4kw in installed capacity that will produce 847×10^8kwh of electricity output annually. This capacity is equal to 6 sets of Gezhouba Project's capacity or 10 sets of Dayawan nuclear power plant.

On the right bank of the dam, there are 6 underground hydraulic turbine generator units. Each set of generator's installed capacity is 70×10^{4x}kw, totaling 420×10^{4x}kw in installed capacity. The input will be finished synchronically with the whole project. These sets of generator units' output capacity are 1.5 times equal to Gezhouba Project's capacity.

The TGP hydraulic power station is installed 32 sets generator units, the single unit is one of the largest generator units around the world. Due to the requirement of flood control and silt flushing, the head fluctuating difference of operation will reach 52m, with the ratio of the maximum head and minimum head. The pool level will reduce from 175m to 145m in flood control. Under the condition of such great water head fluctuation, the design manufacture and installation are more difficult than for any existing large sized generating units.

From environmental protection aspect, TGP will supply 1000×10^8kwh clear power. Compared with the same output thermal power plants, it will equal to the reduction of 5000×10^4 tons raw coal combustion annually, which means 1.2×10^8 tons CO2, 2×10^6 tons SO2, 1×10^4 thousand tons CO, 37×10^4 tons NOx, and a large amount of waste water and solid discharge will be decreased correspondingly. This will be beneficial to improve the environment of middle and east china, especially to prevent acid rain damage and greenhouse affect. This clear and cheap power will support the modernization of China without interval.

TGP power transmission project is an important component of the project. The power station is located in the center of China; it is 500 to 1000 km away from the central China, East China, South China, and North China and east of Sichuan power grid. In this area, the power will be transmitted to all our country with 15 transmission lines, with 500 k VAC lines.

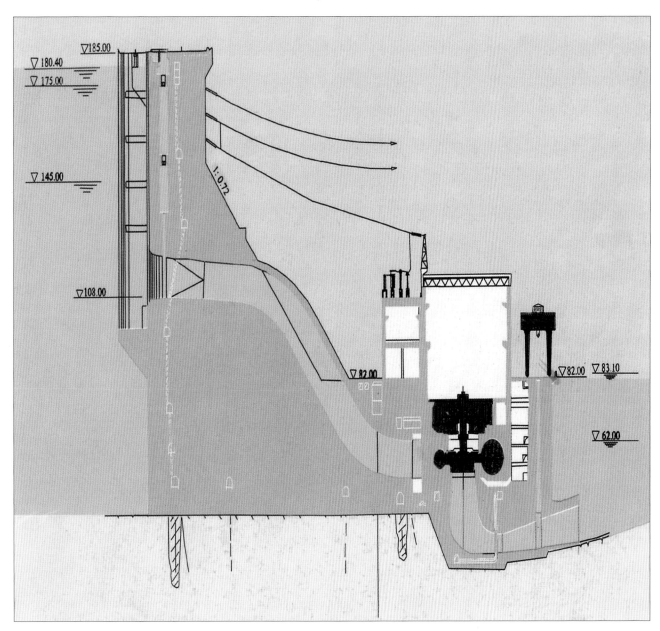

Right Section of the Power Houses

The Installation of Generator Units on the Left Bank Dam

The Installation of Generator Units

Gigantic Turning Wheels Of Hydraulic Power
Plant Are Shipped to the TGP

Left-bank Power Station

Spiral Case of Generators in the TGP

Constructions of the Third Phase of the TGP

Central Control Room of the Power Station

The Generator Units at the
Left Bank Power House

Generating Electricity

Navigation

Compared with the other rivers over the world, before impounding of TGP, the Yangtze River is known as Gold Waterway.

Before impounding of TGP, on 660 km watercourse from Chongqing to Yichang, there are 139 dangerous shoals and rapids, 46 one- way sections, 25 locations where large fully-loaded freighters need winching and the annual one- way shipping capacity is less than 10 million tons. Some of them cannot navigate at night. The difficulty of navigating in this reaches is well known from ancient times. In the year 1981, after using Gezhouba Project, water level raises more than 20 meters and over 100 km's backwater. This inundates 30 dangerous shoal but more than 550 km's watercourse is in original condition. At that time only the ship below 1000ton can sail through the Chuangjiang watercourse. In the dry season every year, because of the small runoff and small water level, only the ship below 1000 ton can go through the middle reaches of the Chuangjiang watercourse. This situation can not match the name of Gold Waterway.

One of functions of TGP is to improve navigation of the Yangtze River. The Three Gorges Reservoir is 660 km long and 101 km wide on average. It covers an area of 1,084 km^2. The efficiency of the carrying capacity will be obviously improved. The ship from lower reaches to upstream will use 1/30 amount of oil that is used before. Because of the reduction of velocity of flow, the ship can sail the whole day. This can reduce the sail time, and reduce coast of navigation by 35% to 37%. The waterway of the Yangtze River is obviously improved. It is possible for 10,000-ton barge fleet to sail upstream directly to Chongqing from Shanghai. With the regulation of the reservoir, the minimum flow downstream of Yichang in the dry season will be increased from the present 3000m^3/s to over 5000 m^3/s, which will obviously improve the navigation condition in the dry season in the middle reach of the Yangtze River.

The navigation facilities of TGP are facilities to deal with the problem of hoe ship sail through TGP. The max. upstream water level of TGP is 175 m, and the miniature water level of down stream of TGP is 60 m. There are 113 meters' distances between them. The permanent shiplock uses 5 stages to disassemble 113 meter's fall. Every line of the shiplock consists of five lock chambers, transportation system, spillway system and strobes. When the shiplock is working, the transportation system connects with upstream, the water flow from upstream into chambers. Then the water level in chambers is equal to the upstream, the spillway system connects with down stream, the water in chambers flow down the water level is equal to down stream. In this way, according to requirement, ships can sail through dam with this shiplock. It will take 160 minutes to sail through the shiplock. If a passenger ship wants to sail through the dam quickly, it can go through by shiplift. The shiplift is like a water elevator. It can handle a 3000-ton passenger ship per time in 30 minutes. The highest elevation is 113 meters. This is the most gigantic and technically complex shiplift around the world.

The five-stage permanent ship locks of the TGP

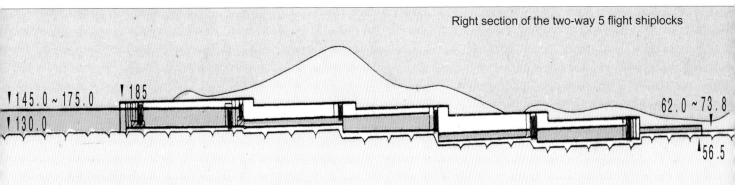

Right section of the two-way 5 flight shiplocks

▼ 145.0 ~ 175.0   ▼ 185   62.0 ~ 73.8 ▼

▼ 130.0   ▲ 56.5

The Five-stage permanent ship locks of the TGP

After the impounding, the river reaches between Yichang and Chongqing with length of 660 km become a gold river route.

The upright shiplift is like a water elevator. It can handle a 3000-ton passenger ship per time in 30 minutes. The highest elevation is 113 meters. This is the most gigantic and technically complex shiplift around the world.

Sketch Map of the Shiplift

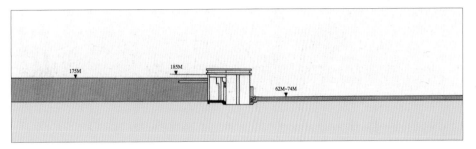

Upright Section of the Shiplift

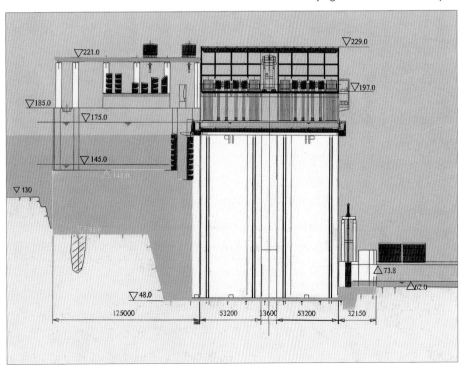

Resettlement

Large amount of relocation and resettlement are of critical importance for the construction of TGP. It is much more difficult than project construction and it is the key issue of project succeeds.

The total land area inundated by the TGP reservoir is 632 km^2, which spread over 20 counties belonging to Chongqing and Hubei. According to the survey which was done by Changjiang Water Resources Commission (CWRC) cooperated with local government concerned, from Oct, 1991 to June, 1992, the TGP reservoir will inundate 2 cities, 11 counties and 116 towns, inundate or influence 1599 enterprises(including 6 large sized and 26 medium sized). It will inundate 24.6 thousand ha farmland (including plantation 17.2 thousand ha and orchard 7.4 thousand ha). It will inundate 824.25 km long road and hydraulic power station with 92.2 thousand KW installed output capacity. It will inundate housing area of 34.596 million m^2 with 846.2 thousand residents living in the inundate area 361.5 of them are farmers. Concerning the increasing of the population and the second time relocation the total population to be relocated will reach 1.13 million.

In order to make sure the smooth carry out of the relocation, 400x10^8 Yuan investment for the resettlement has been approved. It is 45% of the whole project's investment. The static investment of the TGP is 900.9 x10^8 Yuan. The investment of the project itself is 500.9 x10^8 Yuan. The State Council also regulate that after completing the whole project, a portion of profit from power generation will be allocated as development funds to promote local economy in the reservoir region.

The State Council has made series preferential polities one of the most important one is the development oriented resettlement policy. According to this policy, resettle compensation is not a simple compensation by cash; the government should guarantee for the living condition and production ability and promote economic development of the reservoir region to benefit both relocates and hosts. The program should maintain relocatees' living standard and give opportunities for them to achieve a higher standard in future.

The Backout of the Old Zigui County

The New Zigui County

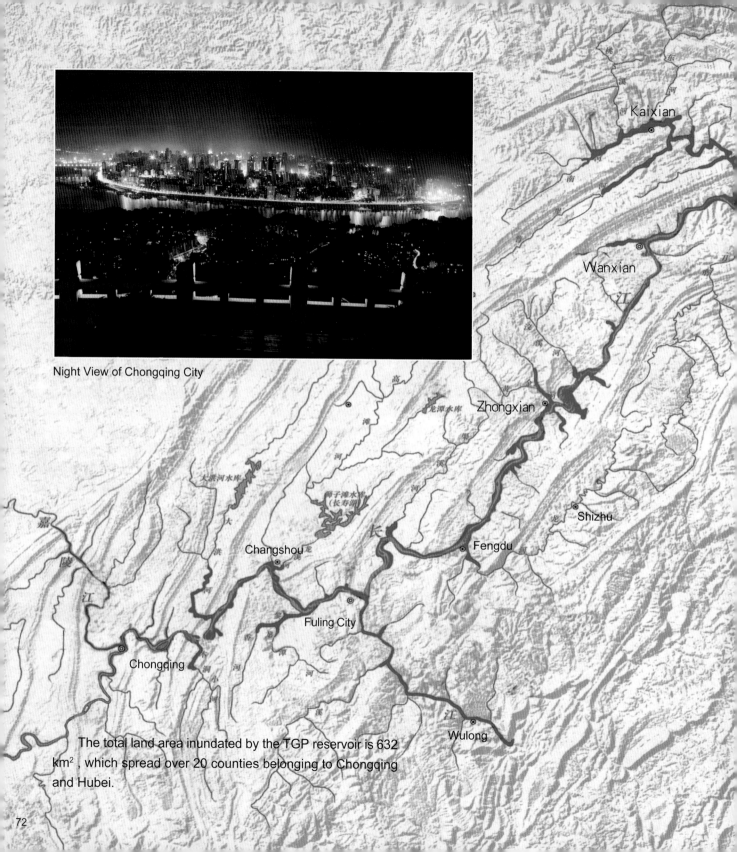

Night View of Chongqing City

The total land area inundated by the TGP reservoir is 632 km^2, which spread over 20 counties belonging to Chongqing and Hubei.

Wushan

Fengjie

Badong

The Three Gorges Project

Zigui

The Gezhouba Project

Yichang

Yichang City —— Capital of Water and Electricity

Removing ShuangLong Town in Wu Mountain

Move out of Home Town with a Bottle of Earth

Removing the Ancient Houses at XiLing Gorge

Sedimentation

Sedimentation issue is one of the most difficult issues in reservoir construction around the world. The Yangtze River has an abundant inflow. according to observation at Yichang the average turbid of the Yangtze River is 1.19 kg/m^3, annual average sediment load coming into the TGP reservoir amounts to 5.3x10^8 tons. If so large amount of sediment is not properly treated, not only the normal benefits will be reduced and the life of reservoir will be shorten, but also the smooth navigation of the main Yangtze River course would be affected.

The reservoir will operate based on an operation manner of "impounding the clear and discharging the turbid". The length of TGP reservoir is over 600 km and the average width is only 1.1 km. It is a lake like reservoir. The dam is equipped with 23 bottom outlets at low elevation(90 m) and large dimension (7 × 9 m). The reservoir's pool level will be kept at low level (145m) during the flood season. This condition will make it feasible for the reservoir to operate based on an operation manner of "impounding the clear and discharging the turbid". In the flood season from June to September, when the inflow carrying 61% of the annual runoff and 84% of annual sediment, the reservoir draws down to flood control level of 145m, which creates a condition in favor of sediment sluicing, allows a huge amount of sediment being discharged out of reservoir through the bottom outlets, causing "discharging the turbid" to be realized. In the end of October, with a decrease in sediment concentration, the reservoir will be impounding up to the normal pool level 175m, causing "impounding the clear" to be realized. With this mode, most of turbid from upstream can be spilled out of the reservoir. Little plain is expected to be formed along the main channel in the reservoir; the effective storage capacity of the reservoir will be permanently reserved. The silt deposition in TGP reservoir has been analyzed numerically by mathematical modeling. According to the calculating result, after approximately 80-100 years of operation when the reservoir sedimentation already come to a balanced state for silt depositing and sluicing, the effective storage capacity of the reservoir will still be kept at 86-92% of the original.

The dams to be built on the upper Yangtze River and its tributaries thereof, and the ongoing water & soil conversancy works and shelter belt forestry scheme are functioning as sediment reduction in the middle and upper valley.

In the flood season from June to Sept, when the inflow carring a great amount of sediment out of the reservoir area.

Silt Sluice

The Menace of War

The TGP reservoir contains $393 \times 10^8 m^3$. If war brakes out, the collapse of the dam will affect the lower reaches or not? How does TGP face menace of war? These issues also attract wide range of attention.

Firstly, TGP have a spillway dam with the greatest ability of flood discharging of the world. If a cataclysm breaks out, to threat the safety of Chuanjiang River or its tributaries, or TGP becomes attract goal of enemy state, all the outlets will be opened, the pool level of the reservoir will decrease to a relatively safe level very quickly. Secondly, China is a country loving peace; we will unit all the peace powers to avoid the war breaking out. Thirdly, modern war always has some sight before breaks out. Before the war, we can operate the reservoir on the war mode; we also can empty the reservoir to make it a power generation station without reservoir. The enemy state's intention to make a disaster in the middle and lower reaches area will be bankrupted. Fourthly, the dam is a concrete gravity dam. It can stand conventional weapons' attacking. TGP is designed based on principle of combining peace and war, and use some methods to improve its anti attack ability, reduce weapons' execution. Fifthly, if TGP collapse by attacked of nuclear weapons, what is the result. The Water Recourses Ministry and CWRC have made some mode experiences based on this kind of situation. There are two disciplinary understanding. The first thing is that in the 20 km's reach between the dam and the Nanjin Pass, there are steep valley bank. This can effectively control the spilled flow, and slow the sluice speed. The second thing is that the sluice is the stored water of the reservoir; associated with the Jingjiang River's plaint area it may affect a local disaster in the upstream area of Jingzhou City. It will not threaten Wuhan. Sixthly, our country is also a great power of nuclear power, our state's anti missile technology is well advanced. We can head off missiles out of the realm. Even it enter into our realm, we have multiple layer to head off. It can be realized to avoid missiles attacking of the TGP.

Geological Issues

1.Reservoir Induced Earthquake

Since 1970s, the reservoir-induced earthquake has become one of major research subjects. More than 100 examples of reservoir induced earthquake around the world have been analyzed. Detailed geological investigations in the reservoir area, which include analyzing of rock characteristics, geological structures and seepage condition, have been made. Rock stress measurement in borehole with depth of 300-800 m and enforced observation to the major faults alongside the dam area has been made. Mathematical analyzes with three dimensions FEM has been used to presume the possibility of the reservoir-induced earthquake. The essential conclusion is that the 16 km valley between the dam site and Miaohe River is crystalline rock. The bedrock of this area is sound and intact. The regional seismic activities are small in intensity, low in frequency. The whole area belongs to a slight seismic area ranking as degree IV of seismic intensity. The bedrock of 142 km reach, from Miaohe River to Baidicheng Town, is carbonate rock. The karst may induce earthquake, but the degree of seismic intensity will below degree IV. The bedrock of upstream of Baidicheng Town is sandstone. In this area, there are no major faults, and no seepage condition. This condition will not make reservoir induce earthquake.

According to the long-term investigation, the earth's crust of TGP's dam and reservoir area is stable. There is no geological background to produce a serious reservoir induced earthquake. After impounding of the reservoir, there is a possibility of induced earthquake to happen, but the highest intensity of the induced earthquake would not be higher than degree VI. Because the designed standard of main structures is supportable an earthquake intensity if degree VII, so the reservoir induced earthquake has no harmful affect to the main structures.

2. Stability of the Bank of the Reservoir

As a result from the investigation during 1950-1970, there is no possibility for the water leakage out of the TGP's reservoir. After two serious landslides happened in Three Gorges river section, Jipazi and Ziguixintan, in the early of 1980s, a comprehensive research of landslide in the reservoir has been executed.

After the special investigation of the Yangtze River and its 173 tributaries, analyzing airscape, 33 serious landslide points' large scale mapping and reconnaissance and mathematical analyzes, a panoramic conclusion has been made. Most of the TGP reservoir bank is composed of hard rock. Few major faults exist and the new tectonic movement is not strong in the reservoir area. So the bank of the reservoir is stable in general. According to the investigation, in the reservoir area, the landslides with a quantity larger than 1×10^6 m^3 have been identified, serious fault rock with a quantity of 284. the total quantity of unstable landslide is only 3.4×10^8m^3, and with a distance to the dam site being over 26 km. After impounding of the reservoir, some of the landslide would be activated but no harmful affect to the navigation and structures would happen.

After impounding of the reservoir, towns and residential areas would have the most harmful affect. So it is important to pay attention to the geological conditions of the new town and residential areas. At the same time, landslide should be inspected.

Lianzi Cliff, the TGP strengthen the bedrock of the cliff and ensure the stability of it.

The Three Gorgers Project Dam Site ——Zhongbaodao Islet, made up of the rigid granite, is the ideal dam site.

The History of TGP Construction

The assumption of improving the navigation condition and exploiting water resource is first issued by Dr. Sun Yat-sen. In the year 1919, he mentioned in his State Founding Plan that improving the watercourse from Yichang to upstream about 100 km. To construct a dam on this section, blast reefs and dangerous shoals, ships can go upwards the city of Chongqing. In August 1924, when he made a speech in National Guangzhou Teaching Training College, he said that water resource in the Kui Gorge of the Yangtze River, and generate over30 thousands KW. This amount of power is more than the power generated by the whole country.

The TGP dream of the Kuomintang government: in October 1932, Resource Commission of the Kuomintang government organized a reconnaissance team to investigate hydraulic power generation on the upstream of the Yangtze River. They spent 2 months in investigating the Three Gorges area, and compiled a report about constructing power station on the river. They chose two places as site of dam. One is HuanglingTemple, the other one is Gezhouba. They suggested that at Gezhouba, the dam can consist of a powerhouse with installed output capacity about 3×10^5KW, and a shiplock. At Huangling Temple, the dam can consist of a powerhouse with installed output capacity about 5×10^5 KW, and a shiplock. The Communication Ministry wrote

back that the plan is clear and it is kept in the archives for future reference.

In the year 1944, the adviser of Wartime Produce Bureau made a suggestion that the government can construct a power station on the Yangtze River with installed output capacity about 1.050×10^7KW. This cheap power can be used to produce fertilizer, and export them to U.S.A. America will provide a loan about 9×10^8 dollars for this project. The loan should be repaid in 15 years.

In May 1944, Resource Commission of the Kuomintang government invited Dr. John Lucian Savage, the American well known dam expert of US Bureau of Reclamation to make a investigation of the Yangtze River. Accompany with engineer from China, he made a preliminary survey, and wrote a preliminary report about a plan on the Three Gorges of the Yangtze River. This report shocked the world. He suggested that a dam can be constructed on the site between Nanjin Pass and Shipai Bay. The crest elevation of the dam is 225 meters. The total installed output capacity is 1050×10^4 KW, with single units of generator 11×10^4 KW. The dam has navigation facilities like shiplock. It is capable of passing 10000 ton barge fleet and sail directly to Chongqing.

In the year 1946, Dr. Savage came to china again, and US Bureau of Reclamation made a agreement of technique cooperation with Resource Commission of

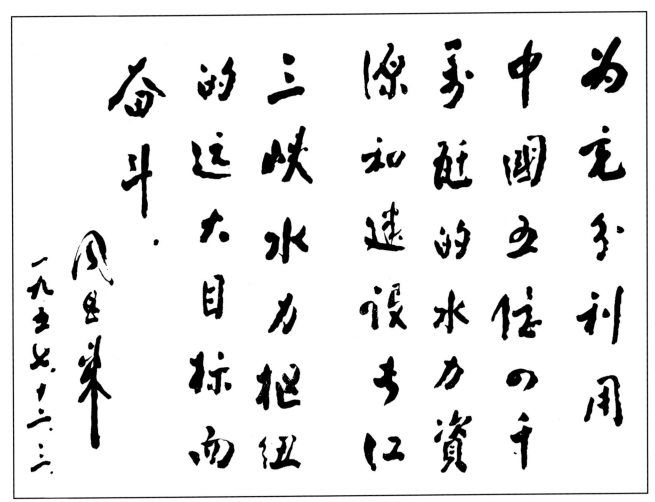

为充分利用中国文化的千千万万的水力资源和建设长江三峡水力枢纽的这大目标而奋斗。

周恩来

一九五七、十二、三

The epigraph written by premier Zhou Enlai:
Working for fully exploiting 5.4x10^8 KW water resources and constructing the Yangtze River Water Conservancy Pivotal Project.   December 3, 1957

the Kuomintang government. 54 technicians were sent to America to design and research on the Three Gorges Project. Dr. Savage once said that the nature condition of the Yangtze River is the best place to build a dam around the world. As the Kuomintang government wanted to make a civil war, the project had to be paused. When he heard this information, he cannot help bursting into tears. When he was old, he said that the Three Gorges was a dream mixed with sweet and suffering. It is the first concrete plan to build a dam on the Yangtze River, through it has a serious disadvantage. In the year 1974, Zhou Enlai commented him fairly that through Dr. Savage is an American, he is a great scientist. He just investigated dam site at Nanjin Bay. He made an assumption to build a dam on the river. On September 23, 1997, before the closure of the river, China Yangtze River Three Gorges Project Development Corporation (CTGPC) and Changjiang Water Resources Commission (CWRC) sent deputy to America to present fresh flowers and a rock from the bedrock of the dam site in front of his tomb.

Since the founding of the P.R. China, the Changjiang Water Resources Commission (CWRC) was established in Feb. 1950 in Wuhan.

In the year 1953, when Mao Zedong debriefed an introduction on the plan of building dams on the Yangtze River and its main tributaries, he suggested to construct a large scale project to completely control flood on the Yangtze River.

In Sep. 1954, the dean of CWRC, Lin Yishan suggested to choose Huangling Temple as dam site. The dam's normal pool level is 191.5 meters.

In July 1956, Mao Zedong wrote a poem to predict the blueprint of the Three Gorges Project.

On December 3, 1957, Premier Zhou Enlai wrote an epigraph for exhibit of nation's water resources construction. He wrote that: working for fully exploiting 540 billion KW water resources and constructing the Yangtze River Water Conservancy Pivotal Project.

In Jan. 1958, in the CPC meeting in Nanning, the supporter, Ling Yishan of TGP and the opponent, Li Rui argued severely in front of Mao Zedong. After he debriefed different suggestions from experts, he made a guide line that is make a positive preparation, and make a precise investigation.

From Feb.26, 1958 to Mar. 5, Premier Zhou with vice Premier Li Fuchun and Li Xinnian organize leaders of provinces around the Yangtze River drainage area and experts from China and Russia, including Lin and Li to made an autoptical trip by ship along the Yangtze River. On Mar. 1, they went to Nanjin Pass Dam site chosen by Dr. Savage, later they went to Zhongbaodao Dam site. When Premier Zhou saw over samples from bedrock, he felt very satisfied the geologic condition of this site. He took one of samples to Chairman Mao. Some experts argued that along the 200 km's Three Gorges reaches are calcareous bedrock; only along the 20 km's reach of Sandouping is intact granite. This site is an ideal site to construct dam. They suggested abandoning investigating the Nanjin Pass dam site. Besides investigating on the spot, Premier Zhou held a meeting with experts to discuss in the ship. After they reached Chongqing, he denoted clearly that experts should put emphasis on researching Sandouping dam site.

On Mar. 30, 1958, Chairman Mao inspected the Yangtze River by ship.

On Apr. 25, 1958, in the CPC meeting in Chengdu, CPC centre committee passed the first document on TGP issues. The main content is that from the aspects of long-term economic goal and technology development, the TGP water conservancy pivotal project is needed and is able to be constructed. The TGP is treated as the back one project of the Yangtze River. A sufficient preparation and concrete guideline should be composed. After that meeting, a leading group was established; nearly 200 units and more than ten thousand researchers took part in TGP research and elementarily designed. After two years' research, they chose Sandouping as its dam site with 200 meters normal pool level, and the capacity of the first group of generator units. They had investigated inundating indices of reservoir area. They made a physical sediment model test.

Because of withdraw of experts from Russia and nature disasters from the year 1959 to 1961, the TGP plan was laid aside.

In the year 1970, after study the relation between TGP and Gezhouba Project, CPC center Committee approved to construct Gezhouba Project, on Dec. 26, 1970. The Gezhouba Project is an important component of the TGP. The construction of this project is to make a technique preparation for the TGP. The Gezhouba Project began to generate power from 1981, and was completed in 1989. This project does not only generate a great amount of power but also improves navigation condition of the Yangtze River. This is a great accomplishment in science and technology. After visit the Gezhouba Project, many experts from abroad said that Chinese people can construct any kind of project, including the TGP, after the Gezhouba project.

In Apr. 1984, the State Council principle approved feasibility report about TGP water conservancy pivotal project. They preliminary confirmed that the dam's normal pool level is 150 meters. In the year 1984 and 1985 a earlier stage preparation of construction was started to prepare a good condition for starting the main component of the project.

At the end of 1984, the CPC committee of Chongqing made a suggestion to centre committee that according to this plan, the water course navigation condition downstream of Chongqing can not be improved. 10000 ton barge fleet can not sail upstream directly to the harbors of Chongqing. They suggest raising the normal pool level to 180 meters. The cost of inundating and resettlement is a little increased but integrative benefit is much more than the cost.

In June 1986, the State Council organized a group of experts to modify the original plan. The Water Resources Ministry established a group lead by Qian Zhengyin to study the new feasibility report and made a conclusion that the TGP is very useful to the Four Modernizations; it is practical in technology, reasonable in economic development. They suggest that the crest

The Statues of Tanziling Crown

elevation of the dam is 185 meters and normal pool level is 175 meters. The plan is one stage of exploitation, several stages of impounding, and series stages of resettlement.

On April 3 of 1992, the fifth session of the 7th National People's Congress passed the resolution on the construction of the Three Gorges Project, with 1761 affirm, 177 veto, 664 disclaim, and 25 absent. This marked the end of the verification phase for ATGP and the commencement if its implementation phase.

In the early of 1993, the construction for the preparatory works started.

On December 14 of 1994, the construction started.

On November 8 of 1997, the closure if the grand channel has been achieved.

In the early of 2003, the dam of the TGP is nearly completed. The TGP reservoir is impounding on April 1. Ten days later the pool level reached 135 meters. Fromthat day on, the Yangtze River is changed fro a river to a lake. On June 16, the double-way 5 flight shiplock trailed to open navigation. The first units of generator began to work on June 24. Once the water of the Yangtze River runs through the dam, it will be transformed to electronic power. When the pool level of the reservoir rise one meter the capacity of the reservoir will increase 4×10^8 m^3, the powerhouse of TGP and Gezhouba Project will increase electronic power nearly 1×10^8 KWH.

The statues of Tanziling Crown:
It tells story about Chinese people fight to change water resources from harm effect to benefit from Dayu thousands years ago. This is the action of fighting against the nature without cowering.

The Gezhouba Project

Gezhouba Dam is an important p[art of the TGP, and it is the first hydraulic power station along the Yangtze River in China. It is located in Yichang City of Hubei Province, and 4 km away from the center of the city, 38 km away from the TGP dam site. It was constructed from December 30, in 1970 and on January 14, 1981, the Yangtze River was enclosured successfully. On December 27, 1981, the first set of generator unit began to work, and in December, 1988, the structure was completed. From that time on the Gezhouba Project produces comprehensive benefits mainly in navigation, flood control power generation, and tourism.

After the Yangtze River running out of the Nanjin Pass, the width of the Yangtze River enwide from 300 meters to 2200 m. Stream of the river is divided into 3 streams by 2 islets in the river, one is Gezhouba the other one is Xiba. The three streams are called Dajaing, Erjiang and Sanjaing from south to north. The Dajiang is the main stream. The water of the Yangtze River will run through the other two streams in Flood Season. The name of the project is from the name of the islet.

The Gezhouba Project is one of the largest hydraulic power stations of the world. The permanent equipments and structures are designed, produced and installed by China. The project consists of dam, 3 shiplocks, 2 power plants, spillway dam with 27 holes, the silt sluice dam of Dajian and the silt sluice of Sanjiang. The dam is 2605. 6 meters long, with the crest at elevation 70 meters. The max. difference between up- and down stream is 27 meters. The designed storage pool level is 60 meters, the store capacity is 15.8x10⁸ m³.

The shiplock of the Gezhouba Project: the No.1 shiplock is located on Dajiang. The chamber of No. 1 shiplock is 280m (length) × 34m (width) × 5.5m (depth). The No. 2 and 3 shiplock are located on Sanjaing. The chamber of them is 280m (length) × 34m (width) × 5m (depth) and 120m (length) × 18m (width) × 3.5m (depth) respectively. The No. 1 and 2 locks are the largest shiplock around the world; they can handle large passenger ship and 10000 ton barge ship fleet. The V-shaped lock gate is 19.7 meters wide, 34 meters long and 2.7 meters thick, the weight of one gate is 600 ton. It will take 51 to 57 minutes for a ship to sail through the shiplock.

The powerhouse of Dajiang has been equipped with 14 units of generators, with a single installed capacity of 12.5x10⁴KW. The powerhouse of the Erjiang has been equipped with 2 units of generator with a single installed capacity of 17x10⁴KW, and 5 units of generators with single installed capacity of 12.5x10⁴ KW. The total installed capacity is 271.5x10⁴ KW and annual output is

The Serenade of Gezhouba Dam

List of Principle Indices of the Gezhouba Project

Item Description	Unit	Index
Drainage Area	km^2	100×10^4
Designed Pool Level	m	66
Crest Elevation	m	70
Total Storage Capacity	m^3	15.8×10^8
Annual Average Runoff	m^3/s	14 300
Designed Flood Runoff (Flood in 1788)	m^3/s	86 000
Check Flood Runoff (Flood in 1870)	m^3/s	110 000
Handled Ship Tonnage of No.1 and No. 2	t	$(1.2 \sim 1.6) \times 10^4$
Handled Ship Tonnage of No.3	t	0.3×10^4
Total Installed output Capacity	kw	271.5×10^4
Annual Average Power Generation	kwh	160×10^8
Max.Flood Sluice of 27 Outlets	m^3/s	83 900
Length of the Axis	m	2 606.5
Concrete Placement	m^3	$1\ 113 \times 10^4$
Earth & rock Excavation and Embankment	m^3	1.113×10^8
Mental Works	t	7.75×10^4

nearly 157×10^8 KWH. The power is transmitted to our country through 220KV AC lines and 500 KV AC lines.

The flood sluice dam is located on Dajiang with 27 outlets, the capacity of flood sluice is 839×10^2 m³/s. The silt sluice dam is located on Erjiang and Sanjiang respectively. The function of these dams is to discharge silt. The capacity of the silt sluice dam with 9 outlets id 2×10^4 m³/s, the dam on Sanjiang is 1.05×10^4 m³/s. When the flood sluice dam and silt sluice dams are opened at the same time, the sluice capacity can reach 11×10^4 m³/s. On July 19, 1981, the 1000-year frequency flood with 7.2×10^4 m³/s, ran through the dam safely.

The Gezhoba Project is the first large scale dam in China along the Yangtze River. It is the regulating reservoir and one of the flight stages of the TGP. After regulating the flood sluice, power generation and navigation, the Gezhouba Project enlarge its output capacity over 4×10^5 KW.

Generate Electricity

Open to Navigation (shiplock)

The Flood Sluice of Gezhouba Dam

A Full View of Gezhouba Dam

Environmental Impact of TGP

There are 47 rare or endangered plant species protected by the nation in the surrounding areas affected by the reservoir, most of them grow between 300 to 1200 m above sea level. There is almost no natural vegetation in the inundated area. The impounding will not cause serious losses.

Totally 26 rare animals of class I and II protected by the nation are living in the remote and mountainous areas and will not be affected by the project. The State Council will establish a serious of nature reserve areas around the reservoir area, such as Tianbaoshan Forest Park, Longmenhe Evergreen Broadleaf Forest Nature Reserve Area, and the Small Three Gorges Zoological Nature Reserve Area. They will facilitate the protection of wild animals and plants around the reservoir area.

The TGP reservoir will have a little affect on Chinese sturgeon, animals of class I protected by the nation, living. The migration of Chinese sturgeon has been blocked from the operation of Gezhouba Project. From the year 1984, hundreds of thousands artificial spawning fish fries have been put into the Yangtze River every year since them and new natural spawning areas area founded down stream. The research of Chinese sturgeon, which includes artificial spawning, breed, and the protection of the new spawning areas will be strengthening.

The habitual of Chinese dolphin is 100 km down stream of TGP, so the construction and operation of TGP will not affect them. But Chinese dolphin is listed as worldwide rare and endangered species and two natural protection areas, Tongling and Shishou, have been establishes in middle and lower reaches of the Yangtze. A long term systematic survey and researches have indicated that the habitats of Yangtze alligator and Siberian crane will not affected.

Peach Fish (Minnow)

Giant salamander

Chinese Sturgeon: it is more than 500 kg weight. It is the oldest amniote that living around the world. It appears from Mesozoic the Cretaceous Period, which is 1.4×10^8 years from today. It was born in Jingshajiang River and grows in the sea. Every autumn, they will spawn in the Yangtze River, and then the fish fries will grow in the sea.

Wood lotus in the year 1907, the British Royal Academic Association organized a group of expert from England, America and France to investigate the Yangtze River. They found this rare plant in Badong County, at the first time. As there existing only 3 plants, so it is treated as living fossil. In the year 1986, government designed a set of memorial stamps about this lotus.

Maidenhair tree, it is one of the oldest spermatophytes that existing on the earth.

A Bird of Minerva

Golden Monkey of Shennong Jia

A Kind of Bird Living in Zigui

Groups of Monkeys in the Three Gorges

Cultural Relic and Historical Site Protection of TGP

The impoundment of the reservoir will affect 44 archaeological sites and ancient monuments. Of them, Baiheliang, the famous ancient low water record tablets near Fuling City, is protected by the nation, other 5 by provinces. The most famous ones however will not be inundated such as Ghost City in Fengdu County, Baidicheng in Fengjie County. Efforts would be made to salvage the cultural heritage that may be inundated. For example, the Baiheliang low water record tablets, Zhangfei Temple, Shibaozhai and Quyuan Temple will be relocated and exhibited in suitable places or will be protected by foundation consolidation and strengthening.

Accompany with the construction of TGP, an unprecedented archaeological discovery started from the year 1995 to the year 2003. experts have excavated in the reservoir area about 900x10^4 m^2. And more than 6000 rare cultural relics are excavated, 60 thousand cultural relics. It includes over 60 Paleolithic sites, and 80 Neolithic sites, over 100 ancient Ba's historical sites and tombs, 470 sites from Han Dynasty to Liuchao Dynasty, nearly 300 sets of ancient architectures including ancestral temples, temples and ancient residences. These historical relics show that the Yangtze River is also a cradle land of Chinese culture.

The Baiheliang Low Water Record Tablets

The Baiheliang low water record tablets are the most important archaeological site of archaeological sites around the TGP reservoir area. Before protection planning of the archaeological sites and ancient monuments, it is put down on the list of the important historical sites to be given special protection by the nation. Baiheliang is located in Fuling City of Chong qing. In the center of the Yangtze River 1 km away upstream of the confluent of the Yangtze River and Wujiang River, there is a rock lying downstream in the center of the river. It is 1600 meters long, 15-20meters wide with an intersection angle being 14.5 degree toward the river center. Before the impounding of the reservoir, its ridge's water level is about 2 meters higher than the average water level of the Yangtze River. So it is submerged by water, only in the year of dry season, its

ridge can be seen in the river. Because the chance of the ridge come out of the water is very limited, if it come out, it is seemed as a luck sign for a harvest in this year.

Stone inscription started from 763 AD. 165 sites have been found on the Baiheliang Low Water Record Tablets. On was carved in Tang Dynasty (618 AD to 907AD), 98 in Song Dynasty (960 AD to 1279AD), 5 in Yuan Dynasty (1206AD to 1638AD), 16 in Ming Dynasty (1368AD to 1644AD), 24 from Qing Dynasty (1616AD to 911AD), and 14 in latter day, 7 carved stone can not trace the date. These stone inscriptions contain more than 30 thousand characteristics. They are carving in different styles. Among these stone inscriptions, there are 14 stone carved fish. One fish is basso-relievo; the other 14 fishes are line engraving. The large one of the ling engraving fish is 1.5 meters long the small one is only 0.3 meters long. This is the sign of the water level in dry season of Tang Dynasty. Another two fishes above this one is made in the year 1685, the average height of the fish abdomen is 137.9 m, which is very closely to the zero sea level that is now used in Fuling hydrology station. These stone fish record the water level of the Yangtze River in the dry season for about 1200 years. It is called the oldest hydrology station along the Yangtze River, a miracle of hydrological history. A hydrology academic meeting hold in 1974 by UNESCO gave a high praise to this creation by ancient people of China.

The TGP reservoir' normal pool level is 175 meters, so this site will be 38 meters under water surface. When in flood season, the pool level decrease to 145 meters, it is sill 8 meters under the water. According to calculating, this site will be buried by silt after the TGP is operated for about 20 years. After research and discussion, experts decided to protect this site by foundation consolidation with non pressure container. According to this plan, a building will be built on this site to protect the stone inscriptions; the building will let water go through it with filter. Then the pressure in and out of the building will establish a dynamic balance. Then a passageway will be built to connect the building and the bank. Passengers can dive into the building to feel this miracle closely with divingde.

Experts of historical sites protection comment that in this way, it is tally with international historical sites protection principles, and protect the site and environment perfectly. This museum under water will be the first museum under water, and it will apply for the list of World' Culture Heritage. There is no country like us to protect cultural heritage perfectly. This site will become one of signs of Fuling City. It will bring a great amount of tourist benefits.

White Crane Ridge at Fuling City

"Ghost City" Fengdu

Fengdu is located on the right bank of the Yangtze River 52km down stream of Fuling City. It is a ghost city with a long history. Why Fengdou is called Ghost City? This is a clerical error in ancient books. It is said that, in the Han Dynasty, two person lived in Pingdu Mountain one was named Yin Changsheng; the other was called Wang Fangping. In the Tang Dynasty, some people told the story that there is a Yinwang (King of Ghost) living in Pingdu mountain. From that time on the town become known as a ghost city. Gradually, more than 70 temples were built in this town, all these temples are related with ghost, such as Yinyangjie (the world and the hell), Naiheqiao (a bridge in the hell that if a person did good things when he is alive, he can pass this bridge, while if a person is very bad when he is alive, he will drop into the river under the bridge and be eaten by beast in it.), Wangxiangtai(a platform ghost can see his hometown), Huhang Hall (a hall that God live in it), and Yuanxiao Hall (a hall above cloud). All these buildings are called the Hell. There are lively statues of god and ghost in these temples. Fengdu become a Buddhism Holy Land. The Pingdu Mountain has changed the name to Mingshan Mountain with Sushi's (a famous poet in Song Dynasty) poem.

It is said that after dying the soul of person will come to Fengdu, and to be judged by the King of Ghost according to their activities of their live. If he is a good person when he is alive, he will be metempsychosis. If he is a cacodemon, he will be sent to the hell. Naihe Bridge is a bridge consists of 3 arches. It is said that this is the first stage to the hell; the river under the bridge is Xuehe pool (a pool be full with blood). Only good person can pass this bridge, or it will drop into the pool and be eaten by monsters in it.

From ancient times, many people come to Fengdu to see nature scene and worship. They have left many poems and calligraphy in this town. The Ghost City cannot be taken place by any other kind of temples.

The nature scene and ghost culture is well known all over the world. Nowadays, Fengdu have equipped much modern equipment such as ropeway in Ming Mountain. A Ghost palace and the biggest statue of King of the Ghost have been built. The tongue of the King is 81 meters long. On March 3 of lunar calendar, Ming Mountain holds a Ghost Festival. At this time people will go to street with a mask. Fengdu become a sight of the Three Gorges' traveling line. It attracts a lot of tourists.

The TGP reservoir's normal pool level is 175 meters. The water will reach the foot of Ming Mountain. The gate of Ghost City is 155 meters over the sea level, so it will removed and rebuilt. The Hell on the mountain will not affect. The Fengdu town will resettled to the south bank of the Yangtze River, Ming Mountain will become an island of lake.

The Sign of the ″GhostCity″

"Ghost City" Fengdu

Shibaozhai Village

This village will become a islet in the center of the river after impounding of the TGP reservoir. It is like a bonsai in the middle of lake.

It is located on the north bank of Yangtze River reach in Zhongxian County of Chongqing. It is one of the eight fantastic buildings over the world. It is called pearl of the Yangtze River. It is a single peak with steep hillside. It is like a jade stamp at the bank of river. Because of this it is called Yuyinshan Mountain (jade stamp). Many poems have described the glory appearance of this village.

It is said that, in the year 1545 AD, some skillful craftsmen wanted to construct a fantastic building on the sidehill. They have discussed for a long time, but they haven't got a satisfied method. One day they saw an eagle circling up and finally flied over the mountain. After seeing that an inspiration heat their mind. They decided to build it according to the features of the hill. This village has a scale in Ming Dynasty, and in Qing Dynasty, it have been enlarged. The building became much more beautiful then before. This village has 12 floors with 56 meters high. Pavilions are built on the hillside. The whole building is chocked without nail. The whole building combines the nature and wonderful artical excelling nature skills harmoniously.

To overlook the village, it is like a beautiful picture. When you enter the village, you will see a stele over the gate. It says go straight upstairs with cloud ladder. When you go upstairs with ladders in the building, you will find that there are windows in every floor, tourists can see scene outside of the building. When you reach the tenth floor, you will come to a group of architectures. In these buildings you can find historical figures in Zhongxian County, with form of statues, poems, pictures, and inscription, such as Ba Manzi, Zhang Fei and Qing Liangyu. When you climb to the top of the village, we can see the green mountains far away from here and ships sailing on the river. You will enjoy this place and don't want to leave.

After impounding in 2009, the reservoir's normal pool level is 175 meters; altitude of the gate of the village is 173.5 meters. It is only 1.5 meters lower than the pool level, but the original underground water altitude is 148 to 158 meters.

Shibaozhai Village at Zhongxian County

The altitude of the Yuyinshan Mountain's bedrock is 7 to 15 meters higher than the original altitude. The underground water altitude will rise to 175 meters after impounding. In order to avoid the destroy bedrock of the village by water, to secure the building on the mountain, and protect the historical site with its nature environment, a concrete cofferdam will be built along the village, and leave an opening with 50 meters wide to facilitate tourist to see the panorama of the village. When the TGP is operated on the level of 175 meters, the gate of the break will be closed to protect the village, while on the level of 145 meters, the gate will be opened.

Shibaozhai Village at Zhongxian County

Zhangfei Temple

Zhangfei Temple is the cultural relic that is moved farthest of all the cultural relics. Its old site was located at the south bank of reach in Yunxian County. It is at piedmont of Feifeng Mountain. It covers an area of 2000 m². It consists of halls and pavilions. It was built 1700 years age. It is said that after Zhangfei was assassinated by his followings Fanjaing and Zhangda, they throw his head into the river, when they heard that Wu hand Shu are making peace. At the same day, an old fish man got a head from the river; he thought it is not a luck sign. He threw it into the river again. At that night, the old man dreamed that Zhangfei is standing on his knees in front of him with tears. He said that I want to help the Han dynasty to be reconstructed. Please get my head out of the river and buried on the land of Shu. The old man was shocked and got up to buried Zhangfei's head at the piedmont of Feifeng Mountain. Local people built a temple to hold a memorial for Zhangfei.

Four large characters written by Peng Juxin were carved on the stone wall facing the river in front of the temple. A famous poet Dufu had stayed here for 2 years, and he wrote over 30 poems. The Zhufeng pavilion was built 850 years age. The existent building of the temple was built in Ming and Qing Dynasty. It covers an area of 1500m². It collects advantages of art of architecture. It is worthwhile to investigating the ancient architecture through this temple. The temple contains many stone inscriptions, calligraphy, and pictures. It is known with three tops. They are top articles, top calligraphy, and top stone inscriptions. It has over 360 engraved inscriptions, 217 woodcutting pictures. Besides the engraved inscriptions, there is a set of bell from Xizhou and a bronze sward from Dongzhou. It also has brick from Han Dynasty, and 350 cultural relics from Neolithic times.

Some of them have a historical value and artistry. On the wall of the temple, there are some lines carved in the Genwu year in Qing Dynasty which record the water level of the flood at that time. At the east side of the temple, there are 170 stone inscriptions on the dragon's ridge stone near the bank of the river. They are rare hydrological information of the Yangtze River.

The altitude of the old temple is between 130 to 160 meters; all the cultural relics have to be moved before the impounding of the reservoir. The new temple will be built with materials from the old one and keep its style in the new temple. Zhangfei statue in the old temple id a pottery one, in the new temple it is made of copper. It is 3.1 meters high, 4 tons weight. It looks more lifelikeness than the ole one. It cost more than 300,000 Yuan. The Yunxian County is completely inundated; the new county is 32 km away from the old one near the upstream of the river. The temple will be moved to Qipan town. This site can constrain the environmental condition of the temple and human culture environment. From the aspect of protecting the temple, this site facilitates to maintain the layout of the old temple and make the temple exists harmoniously with surroundings.

Zhangfei Temple at Yunyang County

The Fossil of the Yunyang Dinosaur Back

The Changes of Natural Sight

The Three Gorges are famous for their grand, rare, and beautiful scene, and cultural heritages, with a total length of 193 km. After impounding of the TGP reservoir, the natural scene is influenced a little. The altitude of peaks on the banks of the river is 800 to 1000 meters. The normal pool level of the reservoir is 175 meters, compare to the original level it is 110 meters higher than before. The water level near the Goddess Peak is 50 meters higher than before. The level near the Kuimen (the gate of Kui) is 40 meters higher than before. Because of this, many shoals and reefs are submerged, many cultural relics are disappear running water slows down its speed. A ribbon like lake replaces the river as the new scene of the Three Gorges.

While, after the Three Gorges become the reservoir area of the TGP, navigation condition is improved. The water of lake flows to every valleys and tributaries. Some nature scene can be fully exploited such as the mini Three Gorges on Dalinghe River, Shennong Book, and Stone forest on Gezihe River, and Baolonghe River. Some scene can be reached by boat instead of waling on rugged road, such as the Heavenly Pit and the Earthly Ditch. Gorges, Lake and TGP become the new Three Gorges of The Three Gorges Tourist Area. The range of the new Three Gorges contains the Gezhouba Project, The TGP, Chongqing, and Shenglongjia area nature reserve area. It will become a new heat tourist area in the near future.

Historical Three Gorges

Photos here were taken at the end of the Qing Dynasty in 1911 by German Diplomatic Envoy Fritz when he was touring by wooden boat from Yichang to Chongqing to take his post in Chengdu.

The Qutang Gorge

Qutang Gorge is famous for its magnificent scene. It is described that the peak connects with the heaven and boat sails in the earth ditch. This gorge is the shortest one of the three gorges, but it the most magnificent one. It extends eastwards from Baidicheng Town, to Daxi Town, with a full length of 8 km. The major peaks of Kuimen are facing each other on both sides, and the river was flanked by steep cliffs and towering peaks, with 100 meters in width. When the runoff is above 5×10^4 m³/s, it has amazing powers to run through the Kuimen gorges. Before the operating the project, when passengers go through it by bout, they felt very horrible. After impounding, the water level will rise 40 meters, the gorges are still magnificent, but the flow becomes slow and calm. The Ancient Plank Roads, the Phoenix- Drinking Spring, and Monk Hung Upside Down on the south bank will be submerged.

On the south bank, there is the Whitewashed Wall. From Song Dynasty onwards, it was covered with a large amount of engraved inscriptions, which is more than hundreds of meters wide and ten meters high. The carved words Kunmen and Qutang strike the eyes most. And one of the most treasured inscriptions is Ode to the Resurgence of the Song. It is 4 meters high and 7 meters wide, contains 980 words the in Chinese calligraphy. The cliff is so high that we have to look up at the words. This makes us admire technology and courage of craftsmen in ancient times to engrave words on the cliff. General Fenyuxiang's poem "go out of the Kunmen and drive the invaders out" is on the cliff. When tourists see these words, every one has feeling to protect our hometown.

The methods have been planned to protect these engraved inscriptions. All of the inscriptions are made rubbings, and copy them on the cliff with altitude of 210 meters, 700 meters on the down stream of the old site. Some rare inscriptions are incised, and preserved in the Three Gorges Museum in Chongqing. Some are moved to the new site, some are protected on the old site.

Baidicheng Town is one of the famous historical sites in the Three Gorges at the entrance of Qutang Gorge. The most of it scenes are located on the top of the hill with altitude of 230 meters. After impounding, it will become a islet in the center of the river.

The Precipitous Qutang Gorge

The Magnificent Qutang Gorge

The Stone Inscription in the Three Gorges

Grand Kuimen

The Wu Gorge

Wu Gorge is named after its mountain Wu, and is famous for its beautiful scene. It is flanked with towering peaks and steep cliff. Downstream you have to go through countless twist and turns. The river now seems to be blocked by the huge mountains, now breaks through and changes its direction. It extends from the mouth of Daling River in Wushan County of Chongqing City in the west, and ends at Guandukou (official ferry) in Badong county of Hubei Province in the east, with a length of 50 km. The Twelve Peaks of Mt. Wu is towering and graceful and shrouded with varied and fantastic shaped clouds formed by mist. It is really a poetic picture.

The most famous Goddess Peak is 922 meters higher than the sea level, after impounding there are 747 meters above the water. The small Three Gorges consists of Dicui Gorge, Bawu Gorge and Longmen Gorge, with the length of 50 km. The waterway is narrow; it has riptide and adlittoral water. Tourists think that the small three gorges are different from the Three Gorges and better. From 1980s, the small three gorges are more attractive then the Three Gorges. As the peaks are not so high like the Three Gorges, when boats are sailing on the Daling River, you will nit feel sailing in the valley. After rising of the water level, the scene of Madu River, the branch of Daling River, become more loneness. A mini three gorges are brought to the front of tourists. Shennong Brook, facing to Badong County, is originated from Shennong Jia. At that area, it is full of green trees and beautiful flowers. Before impounding, the brook has many shoals and reefs. It is difficult to go further into the valley. Now tourist can drift on the brook and go straight to Shennong Jia by boat, to discover desolation of virgin forest. Shennv Brook is opposite to Goddess Peak. It has beautiful scene with many beautiful stories. Three peaks of Twelve Peaks of Mt. Wu are in this valley. They are Qiyun Peak (the Rising Cloud Peak), Shangsheng Peak (the Ascent Peak), and Jingtan Peak (the Purity Temple Peak). After impounding, tourist can go into the brook directly by boat.

► The Autumn of Wu Gorge

The ancient plank roads are more than 60 km long and 2~3 meters wide, tens of meters above the water. When walker walk on it, he will feel very horrible.

Stones for Boat Tracking

►

Swarthy back, string like cordelle, stones for boat tracking, trace marks, and ancient plank roads tell us that navigate in the Yangtze River is very difficult in ancient times.

The Xiling Gorge

The Xiling Gorge, which is the longest one of the three Gorges, stretches from the mouth of Fragrance Brook in Zigui County of Hubei Province in the west to the Nanjin Pass of Yichang City in Hubei Province in the east, with a total length of 76 km. The Xiling Gorge had been well known for its numerous shoals and swift torrents. The Qintan Shoal, Konglingtan Shoal used to be the most dangerous shoals in the navigation history of the Three Gorges. But since the completion of the Gezhouba Dam Water Conservancy Pivotal Project, these dangerous shoals of the old days have disappeared once and for all. After impounding the water level will rise over 100 meters. This will have a little harm affect to Bingshubaojian Gorges (military book and sward gorge). The military book and sward like things are coffins placed in the precipices. These coffins are preserved in Quanyuan Temple. The height of ox liver and horse lung of the Ox Liver and Horse Lung Gorge will be submerged. The stone of ox liver and horse lung will be cut and preserved in new Zigui County. There is a clear brook in Xingshan County of Hubei Province. It is know as small

Lijiang River. Because of inconvenient communication, few tourists came to the Fragrant Brook. After impounding, tourist can go to Gaogang Scene Area from the mouth of the Fragrant Brook by boat.

Feilai Temple

Xiling Gorge

A Bird's -eye View of Xiling Gorge

The Beautiful New Three Gorges

The new Three Gorges consists of steep gorges, Peace Lake and the Three Gorges Project. After impounding of the TGP reservoir, the scene is still beautiful. The magnificent Qutang Gorge is still magnificent, Baidicheng becomes a islet of the lake, art gallery like the Xiling Gorge are still shrouding with clouds, goddess are still standing at the bank of the river with dignity and polish. The scene of Xinling Gorge is the best of the world; the Three Gorges Project is the greatest of the world.

Xiling Gorge

The TGP reservoir area after impounding

The Qutang Gorge After Impounding

Baidicheng Town is one of the famous historical sites in the Three Gorges at the entrance of Qutang Gorge. The most of it scenes are located on the top of the hill with altitude of 230 meters. After the water level goes to 175 m, it will become a islet in the center of the river.

The Gate of Baidicheng Town

Star Watch Pavilion

The Hall of Entrustment
of Liu Bei

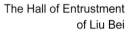

The Cave of Seven Doors

The Wu Gorge After Impounding

The Clouds and Drizzle Around Mt. Wu

A Bird´s - eye View of Wu Gorge

Night Sail in Three Gorge

The Goddess Brook

The Goddess Peak

Nanjin Pass, magnificently located at the mouth of Xiling Gorge, is the end of the Three Gorges, echoing Kui Gate in the west. Flanked by perpendicular cliffs, it seems to be a big bottleneck checking the waters in the river. As soon as it leaves the Nanjin Pass, the Yangtze River flows into the boundless plain of its lower reaches, expanding its width from 300 meters into 2 200 meters. From that point on, it begins to put on a different appearance, as well as to display a different charm, rolling restless in its prolonged eastwards journey into the sea.

Early Spring in Xiling Gorge

圖書在版編目(CIP)數據

宏偉的三峽工程:英文／李金龍主編.
—鄭州:黃河水利出版社,2005.3 (2007.4 重印)
ISBN 978-7-80621-894-5

Ⅰ.宏···Ⅱ.李···Ⅲ.三峽工程－畫冊Ⅳ.TV632.71-64

中國版本圖書館CIP數據核字(2005)第012715號

責任編輯:武會先
責任校對:蘭文峽
責任監製:常紅昕
裝幀設計:李金龍
攝　　影:王連生　王緒波　鄧忠富　何懷强
　　　　　陳　偉　李金龍　徐光萱　簡　易
篆　　刻:蔡静安
版　　畫:徐　水
英文翻譯:翁　磊

宏偉的三峽工程　　　　李金龍主編
_____

出版發行:黃河水利出版社
　　　　　地址:河南省鄭州市金水路11號
　　　　　郵政編碼:450003
發行單位:黃河水利出版社
　　　　　發行部電話及傳真:0371-6022620
　　　　　E-mail: yrcp@public.zz.ha.cn
承印單位:中華商務聯合印刷(廣東)有限公司
設　　計:中華商務設計中心
開　　本:889mm × 1194mm　　1/20
印　　張:7　印數:1 — 1000
版　　次:2007年4月第2版
印　　次:2007年4月第1次印刷
_____
書　　號:ISBN 978-7-80621-894-5/TV·393　　　　定價:120.00圓